Monograph Book

PARENTAL RELATIONSHIP IN BLOOD GROUPING

Editor

Dr. P. Saranraj

Head, Department of Microbiology, Sacred Heart College (Autonomous), Tirupattur, Tamil Nadu, India.

Published by

JPS Scientific Publications
India

Published by

JPS Scientific Publications, Tamil Nadu, India.
E.mail: jpsscientificpublications@gmail.com
Website: www.jpsscientificpublications.com

Published in India.

International Standard Book Number (ISBN): 978-81-943168-2-4

ISBN: 978-81-943168-2-4

ABOUT THE EDITOR – Dr. P. Saranraj

Dr. P. Saranraj is presently an Assistant Professor and Head at the Department of Microbiology, Sacred Heart College (Autonomous), Tirupattur, Tamil Nadu, India. Prior to this he has worked as a Senior Research Fellow in Department of Microbiology, Annamalai University for 3 years. He is having teaching experience of 5 years and he has guided 8 M.Sc students for their project. He has been involved with teaching and research in area of Microbiology and Biochemistry. He received his Ph.D Microbiology degree from Annamalai University in 2013 and he was qualified in NET exam in 2017. He has published 148 papers (Citations – 1868, H - index: 25 and i10 index - 56) in peer reviewed International Journals, 43 Books and 6 Book chapters. He is an Editorial Board Member and Reviewer of 30 International Journals. In the year 2018, Microbiologists Society of India has appointed him as a Coordinator for its Tamil Nadu Division. He has received awards like Best Review Paper Award (2011), Young Scientist Award (2013), Best Research Forum Coordinator Award (2017), Highest Book Publication Award (2017), Best Review Paper Award (2017), Highest Research Paper Publication Award (2018), Young Researcher Award (2018), Best Research Forum Coordinator Award (2019), Indian Microbiologists Society Young Scientist Award (2019) and Highest Citations Award (2019).

Contents

1
INTRODUCTION

The ABO blood grouping system was discovered by the Austrian Biologist Karl Landsteiner in the year 1901. In this ABO blood grouping system, there are eight different types of Blood groups. The Blood groups are differentiated from each other by the antigen which is present on Red Blood Cells (RBCs). The person who has Antigen 'A' on his RBC has the Blood group 'A'. If the person has the Antigen 'B' on his Red Blood Cells has the Blood group 'B'. If the person has both Antigens 'A' and 'B' on his RBCs has the Blood group 'AB'. If both 'A' and 'B' Antigens are absent on the Red Blood Cells, the person has the Blood group 'O'. In the year 1930, Karl Landsteiner and Alexander S. Wiener jointly discovered the Rh factor on RBCs. his blood group (Qadir and Malik, 2010).

The ABO blood grouping system was controlled by the gene which encoding an enzyme Glycosyltransferase which was observed in three allelic forms *viz.*, IA, IB and IO where the two alleles IA and IB are co-dominant and both are dominant over the IO (Kaur *et al.*, 2011), and 4 possible phenotypes *viz.*, A, B, AB and O. The global distribution of the different phenotypes of this blood grouping system varies among the nature of ethnic groups and geographic regions (Choudhury *et al.*, 2014).

The research about the parental relationship of ABO blood grouping and Rh typing in India and its regions, particularly Tamil Nadu was relatively rare (Garg *et al.*, 2015). According to the Mendelian genetic basis and laws, the various types of blood groups are inherited which are shaped by the laws and social processes,

especially regarding the relations between ethnic groups and classes. So, it is very essential for us to be clear about the development process and the population structure in different historical moments if anybody wants to recognize the dynamics in terms of the distribution of the frequency of ABO blood groups (Eru *et al.*, 2014). The present study was aimed to study the relationship between parents and child Blood group in Department of Biochemistry, Sacred Heart College (Autonomous), Tirupattur, Tamil Nadu, India.

OBJECTIVES OF THE PRESENT STUDY

1) Collection of Blood group details of Parents and Students in Department of Biochemistry, Sacred Heart College (Autonomous), Tirupattur.

2) The analyze the Percentage matching of Blood group between the Parents and Children

       (i) Class wise

       (ii) Gender wise

2
REVIEW OF LITERATURE

The discovery of the ABO blood group, over 100 years ago, caused great excitement. Until then, all blood had been assumed to be the same, and the often tragic consequences of blood transfusions were not understood. As our understanding of the ABO group grew, not only did the world of blood transfusion become a great deal safer, but scientists could now study one of the first human characteristics proven to be inherited. A person's ABO blood type was used by lawyers in paternity suits, by police in forensic science, and by anthropologists in the study of different populations.

The ABO blood group antigens remain of prime importance in transfusion medicine - they are the most immunogenic of all the blood group antigens. The most common cause of death from a blood transfusion is a clerical error in which an incompatible type of ABO blood is transfused. The ABO blood group antigens also appear to have been important throughout our evolution because the frequencies of different ABO blood types vary among different populations, suggesting that a particular blood type conferred a selection advantage (e.g., resistance against an infectious disease). However, despite their obvious clinical importance, the physiological functions of ABO blood group antigens remain a mystery. People with the common blood type O express neither the A nor B antigen, and they are perfectly healthy. Numerous associations have been made between particular ABO phenotypes and an increased susceptibility to disease. For example, the ABO phenotype has been linked with stomach ulcers (more common in group O

individuals) and gastric cancer (more common in group A individuals). Another observation is that individuals with blood type O tend to have lower levels of the von Willebrand Factor (vWF), which is a protein involved in blood clotting.

Human blood group antigens are glycoproteins and glycolipids expressed on the surface of red blood cells and a variety of human tissues, including the epithelium, sensory neurons, platelets and the vascular endothelium. Accumulating evidence indicate that ABO blood type is implicated in the development of a number of human diseases, including cardiovascular and neoplastic disorders.

2.1. HISTORY OF BLOOD GROUPING

At the beginning of the 20th century an Austrian scientist, Karl Landsteiner, noted that the RBCs of some individuals were agglutinated by the serum from other individuals. He made a note of the patterns of agglutination and showed that blood could be divided into groups. This marked the discovery of the first blood group system, ABO, and earned Landsteiner a Nobel Prize.

Landsteiner explained that the reactions between the RBCs and serum were related to the presence of markers (antigens) on the RBCs and antibodies in the serum. Agglutination occurred when the RBC antigens were bound by the antibodies in the serum. He called the antigens A and B, and depending upon which antigen the RBC expressed, blood either belonged to blood group A or blood group B. A third blood group contained RBCs that reacted as if they lacked the properties of A and B, and this group was later called "O" after the German word "Ohne", which means "without". The following year the fourth blood group, AB, was added to the ABO blood group system. These RBCs expressed both A and B antigens.

In 1910, scientists proved that the RBCs antigens were inherited, and that the A and B antigens were inherited codominantly over O. There was initially some confusion over how a person's blood type was determined, but the puzzle was solved in 1924 by Bernstein's "three allele model".

The ABO blood group antigens are encoded by one genetic locus, the ABO locus, which has three alternative (allelic) forms - A, B, and O. A child receives one of the three alleles from each parent, giving rise to six possible genotypes and four possible blood types (phenotypes).

2.2. BLOOD GROUPS

The term "blood group" refers to the entire blood group system comprising red blood cell (RBC) antigens whose specificity is controlled by a series of genes which can be allelic or linked very closely on the same chromosome. "Blood type" refers to a specific pattern of reaction to testing antisera within a given system. Over a period of time, our understanding on blood groups has evolved to encompass not only transfusion-related problems but also specific disease association with RBC surface antigens. Karl Landsteiner has been credited for the discovery of ABO blood group system in 1900 (Owen, 2000). His extensive research on serology based on simple but strong scientific reasoning led to identification of major blood groups such as O, A, and B types, compatibility testing, and subsequent transfusion practices. He was awarded Noble Prize in 1930 for this discovery. His obituary lists an immense contribution of more than 346 publications. Later, Jan Jansky described classification of human blood groups of four types.

At present, 33 blood group systems representing over 300 antigens are listed by the International Society of Blood Transfusion (Logdberg *et al.*, 2005; Logdberg *et al.*, 2011). [Most of them have been cloned and sequenced. The genes of these blood group systems are autosomal, except XG and XK which are X-borne, and MIC2 which is present on both X and Y chromosomes. The antigens can be integral proteins where polymorphisms lie in the variation of amino acid sequence (e.g., Rhesus [Rh], Kell), glycoproteins or glycolipids (e.g., ABO).

2.2.1. ABO System

Among the 33 systems, ABO remains the most important in transfusion and transplantation since any person above the age of 6 months possess clinically significant anti-A and/or anti-B antibodies in their serum. Blood group A contains antibody against blood group B in serum and vice-versa, while blood group O contains no A/B antigen but both their antibodies in serum.

2.2.2. H – Antigen

H-antigen is the precursor to the ABO blood group antigens. It is present in all RBCs irrespective of the ABO system. Persons with the rare Bombay phenotype are homozygous for the H gene (HH), do not express H-antigen on their RBCs. As H-antigen acts as precursor, its absence means the absence of antigen A and B. However, the individuals produce isoantibodies to H-antigen as well as to antigens A and B.

2.2.3. Rhesus system

Rhesus-system is the second most important blood group system after ABO. Currently, the Rh-system consists of 50 defined blood group antigens out of which only five are important. RBC surface of an individual may or may not have a Rh

factor or immunogenic D-antigen. Accordingly, the status is indicated as either Rh-positive (D-antigen present) or Rh-negative (D-antigen absent). In contrast to the ABO system, anti-Rh antibodies are, normally, not present in the blood of individuals with D-negative RBCs, unless the circulatory system of these individuals has been exposed to D-positive RBCs. These immune antibodies are immunoglobulin G (IgG) in nature and hence, can cross the placenta. Prophylaxis is given against Rh immunization using anti-D Ig for pregnant Rh-negative mothers who have given birth to Rh-positive child.

2.2.4. MNS antigen system

MNS antigen system, first described by Landsteiner and Levine in 1927 is based on two genes: Glycophorin A and Glycophorin B. The blood group is under control of an autosomal locus on chromosome 4 and also under control of a pair of co-dominant alleles LM and LN. Anti-M and anti-N antibodies are usually IgM types and rarely, associated with transfusion reactions.

2.2.5. Lutheran system

Lutheran system comprised of four pairs of allelic antigens representing single amino acid substitution in the Lutheran glycoprotein at chromosome 19. Antibodies against this blood group are rare and generally not considered clinically significant.

2.2.6. Kell system

These erythrocyte antigens are the third most potent immunogenic antigen after ABO and Rh system, and are defined by an immune antibody, anti-K. It was first noticed in the serum of Mrs. Kellacher. She reacted to the erythrocytes of her newborn infant resulting in hemolytic reactions. Since then 25 Kell antigens have

been discovered. Anti-K antibody causes severe hemolytic disease of the fetus and newborn (HDFN) and haemolytic transfusion reactions (HTR).

2.2.7. Duffy system

Duffy-antigen was first isolated in a patient called Duffy who had haemophilia. It is also known as Fy glycoprotein and is present in the surface of RBCs. It is a nonspecific receptor for several chemokines and acts as a receptor for human malarial parasite, *Plasmodium vivax*. Antigens Fya and Fyb on the Duffy glycoprotein can result in four possible phenotypes, namely Fy (a+b−), Fy (a+b+), Fy (a−b+), and Fy (a−b−). The antibodies are IgG subtypes and can cause HTR.

2.2.8. Kidd system

Kidd antigen (known as Jk antigen) is a glycoprotein, present on the membrane of RBCs and acts as a urea transporter in RBCs and renal endothelial cells. Kidd antibodies are rare but can cause severe transfusion reactions. These antigens are defined by reactions to an antibody designated as anti-Jk^a, discovered in the serum of Mrs. Kidd who delivered a baby with HDFN. Jk^a was the first antigen to be discovered by Kidd blood group system, subsequently, two other antigens Jk^b and Jk3 were found.

Agarwal *et al.* (2013) carried out a study on automated analysis of blood groups in north Indian donor population and observed that the common blood groups in order of frequency were B, O, A, and AB; 94.4% being Rh-positive. In minor blood groups, the most commonly appearing phenotypes were Le (a−b−) for Lewis, Fy(a+b+) for Duffy, Jk(a+b+) for Kidd, and M+N+ for MNS system.

2.3. IMPORTANCE OF BLOOD GROUPS

2.3.1. Structural Lesions of Red Blood Cells

Of the 33 blood group system antigens, five are defined by their carbohydrate structures (ABO, H, P1Pk, I, GLOB); two are obtained from the plasma (LE, CH/RG). The remaining 23 are characterized by the protein sequence of the RBC membrane protein (Daniels and Reid, 2010; Anstee, 2011), five major proteins (DI, Rh, RhAG, MNS, GE, and CO) among them are expressed at higher levels and function as membrane transporters, whereas the functional importance of rest of 17 antigens is unknown. The proposed function of other antigens are mostly receptor/ligand signaling, enzymatic activity, and glycocalyx formation (Denomme, 2004). The null phenotype of the system, however, shows no immune system abnormalities when compared with mice except for a blunted neutrophil response on exposure to bacterial Lipopolysaccharides (Rao *et al.*, 1991). Similarly, Knops blood group antigen has been associated with complement receptor 1 (Luo *et al.*, 2000) and Cromer system with decay acceleration factor (Telen *et al.*, 1988).

2.3.2. Blood groups and Disease association

The ABO blood groups have a profound influence on haemostasis (Zhang *et al.*, 2012). They exert major quantitative effects on plasma levels of von Willebrand factor and factor VIII. Increased association of myocardial infarction, ischemic stroke, and venous thromboembolism is seen with blood groups A and AB (Wiggins *et al.*, 2009) possibly through functional ABO glycol transferases modulation of thrombosis. A higher risk of cerebral venous thrombosis has been reported in Non-O groups (Tufana *et al.*, 2009). Significant association of ABO groups with the prevalence of preeclampsia has been reported, where AB group was found to be associated with an increased risk of 2.1-folds (Hiltunen *et al.*, 2009). Preliminary studies suggested an association of ABO system with malignancies. A positive

correlation has been shown between blood group A with chronic hepatitis-B infection and pancreatic cancer (Wang *et al.*, 2012) and blood group B with ovarian cancer (Gates *et al.*, 2011). Protection against falciparum malaria can be achieved with group O by reducing rosette formation (Anstee, 2010). Blood group O increases the severity of infection in Vibrio cholerae strains (O1 El Tor and O139).

2.4. BLOOD REQUISTION

After the decision to transfuse blood is taken the next step should be to order a requisition during which the following steps need to be remembered.

2.4.1. Blood grouping and cross-matching

The most fatal of all transfusion-related reaction is ABO incompatibility causing complement-mediated intravascular hemolysis. Hence, correct blood grouping and typing, and cross-checking with the blood requisition form is of utmost importance. ABO typing is carried out by testing RBCs for the A and B antigens and the serum for the A and B antibodies before transfusion. The next step involves Rh typing with only 15 % of the population being Rh-negative.

2.4.2. Antibody screening

Here, commercially prepared RBCs with all the antigens, which direct production of antibodies causing hemolytic reactions, are mixed with the recipient's serum to detect the presence of those very antibodies. It is also carried out with the donor's serum.

2.5. CHANGING PRACTICES IN BLOOD GROUPING

There are controversies regarding the best method for procurement of blood during elective and emergency situations: (a) It can be done by routinely asking for grouping and cross-matching in elective surgical patients. Many scientific articles disputed the relevance of preoperative arrangement of blood in surgeries where blood loss is not anticipated to be significant (Ontani and Lilly – Tariah, 2013). (b) Blood may be ordered without full set of investigations (Miller, 2010). ABO-Rh typing alone results in a 99.8 % chance of a compatible transfusion. Antibody screening increases this safety margin up to 99.94 %, and an additional cross-match further increases the compatibility to 99.95 %. In absence of cross-matching, there is a possibility of missing the antigens on donor cells, but in clinical practice, they are of less importance. Hence, "screening and typing" alone should be carried out. Other methods include "type and partial cross-match," which includes the immediate phase of cross-match; "type and uncross match," for those recipients who have never been transfused before, the chance of detection of antibody with each cross-match is 1:1000; "type O Rh-negative uncross match," it is performed in emergency situation when the time for these procedures is limited. In the latter condition, type O Rh-negative packed RBCs, that is, the universal donor can be used as they will have a negligible amount of hemolytic anti-A/anti-B antibodies against the recipient RBCs.

2.6. CURRENT TRENDS AND FUTURE AREAS OF BLOOD GROUPING RESEARCH

Three main antigen-modulation strategies have been proposed to prevent immune recognition of incompatible RBCs and to avoid haemolytic reactions due to alloimmunization. The first approach relies on enzymatic conversion of specific blood group antigens, that is, manipulation of the ABO system. Goldstein and Lenny achieved a remarkable milestone with the development of technology named

"enzyme converted group O-RBC (ECO-RBC) concept" where the B antigen is replaced with O using galactosidase (Goldstein *et al.*, 1982). This treatment leaves fewer than 2000 antigenic sites per RBC without affecting membrane deformability, gas exchange, or expression of the RhD, C and E, MNS, Lewis, Kell, Lutheran, Duffy, and Kidd blood group systems as their antigenicity do not depend on the terminal galactose residues. In contrast with the B antigen, enzymatic conversion of A antigen was difficult due to existence of two Type-A blood group structures (A2 and A1) (Goldstein, 1989). Two new enzymes, N-acetylgalactosaminidase and a-galactosidase have been identified for removal of antigens A and B, respectively; and tested for their ability to generate ECO-RBCs from A1, A2, B, or AB donor units (Liu *et al.*, 2007). The enzyme conversion strategy has also been proposed to resolve ABO incompatibility issues in the field of organ transplantation (Kobayashi *et al.*, 2007). The second approach is to mask antigens by treatment of RBCs with polyethylene glycol; also known as the stealth RBC concept. The third approach involves *in vitro* production of RBCs with a predefined antigenic profile from genetically manipulated stem cells (Hashemi-Najafabadi *et al.*, 2006). Such cells could be used for the generation of "universal-donor" RBCs.

International Society of Blood Transfusion has recently recognized 33 blood group systems. Apart from ABO and Rhesus system, many other types of antigens have been noticed on the red cell membranes. Blood grouping and cross-matching is one of the few important tests that the anaesthesiologist orders during perioperative period. Hence, a proper understanding of the blood group system, their clinical significance, typing and cross-matching tests, and current perspective are of paramount importance to prevent transfusion-related complications. Nonetheless, the knowledge on blood group system is necessary to approach blood group-linked diseases which are still at the stage of research.

Currently, our knowledge on blood groups goes beyond the usual tests of agglutination and transfusion to the better understanding of RBC antigens in light of their association with multiple diseases and the scope of use of this knowledge to modulate the disease processes. In this context, the role of adequate understanding of screening, typing, and cross-matching apart from awareness on evolving trends, for every clinician, may not be overemphasized.

3
METHODOLOGY

The present survey was conducted in the Department of Biochemistry, Sacred Heart College (Autonomous), Tirupattur, Vellore district, Tamil Nadu, India. The survey was conducted during February 2019. Totally, 150 Biochemistry students from six classes (I B.Sc Biochemistry, II B.Sc Biochemistry, III B.Sc Biochemistry, I M.Sc Biochemistry, II M.Sc Biochemistry and PGDMLT) are involved in this present survey. A questioner was prepared and it contains

a) Name of the student
b) Student Blood group
c) Student's father name
d) Student's father Blood group
e) Student's mother name
f) Student's mother Blood group

The Percentage matching of Blood group between the Parents and Children was analyzed in Class wise and Gender wise.

4

RESULTS AND DISCUSSION

4.1. NUMBER OF STUDENTS INVOLVED IN PRESENT RESEARCH

The present study was designed to study the relationship between Parents and Children Blood Group in Department of Biochemistry, Sacred Heart College (Autonomous), Tirupattur, Vellore district, Tamil Nadu, India. The present research is completely a Statistical survey. Totally, 150 students are involved in the present survey. From that 150 students, 50 students are Male and 100 students are Female (Table – 1).

Table – 1: Number of students involved in present research

1	Total number of students involved in Present research	150
2	Males	50
3	Females	100

4.2. DETAILS OF STUDENTS BLOOD GROUPS

The Blood groups of the Biochemistry students in our Sacred Heart College was collected from the students and the data was furnished in Table – 2. Among the eight Blood groups, maximum recorded Blood group among the Biochemistry department students was "O - Positive" (51 students) followed by "B - Positive" (49 students), "B - Positive" (31 students), "AB - Positive" (9 students), "O - Negative" (7 students), "B - Negative" (2 students) and "A - Negative" (1 student). In our survey, we did not find any students with "AB - Negative" Blood group. Comparatively, Positive Rh Typing of Blood groups are observed more when compared to the Positive Rh Typing Blood groups.

4.3. GENDER WISE DETAILS OF STUDENTS BLOOD GROUPS

The Gender wise details of Students Blood Group were analyzed and the findings were given in Table – 3. For male students, highest percentage of Blood group was recorded as "O – Positive" (40 %) followed by "B – Positive" (36 %), "A – Positive" (18 %), "AB – Positive" & "O – Negative" (6 %) and "A – Negative & B – Negative" (2 %). The Blood group "AB – Negative" was not observed in the Male students. For Female students, highest percentage of Blood group was recorded as "B – Positive" (36 %) followed by "O – Positive" (33 %), "A – Positive" (22 %), "AB – Positive" (6 %), "O – Negative (2 %) and B – Negative" (1 %). The Blood group "AB – Negative" and "A – Negative" was not observed in the Female students of Biochemistry department.

4.4. PARENTAL MATCHING OF BLOOD GROUP BETWEEN THE PARENTS AND CHILDREN IN CLASS WISE

Parental matching of Blood group between the Parents and Children in Class wise was studied in the present survey and the results are showed in Table – 4. Among the 150 surveyed Biochemistry students, 88 student (58.66 %) blood group are matched with Mother's blood group, 46 student (30.66 %) blood group are matched with Father's blood group and 16 student (10.66 %) blood group are neutral not matched with Father and Mother blood group.

Table – 2: Details of Students Blood Groups

S.No	Blood Groups	Number of Students
1	'A' +ve	31
2	'B' +ve	49
3	'AB' +ve	9
4	'O' +ve	51
5	'A' –ve	1
6	'B' –ve	2
7	'AB' –ve	-
8	'O' -ve	7
Total number of students		**150 Students**

Table – 3: Gender wise details of Students Blood Groups

S.No	Blood Groups	Gender and Blood group percentage	
		Male	Female
1	'A' +ve	9 (18 %)	22 (22 %)
2	'B' +ve	13 (36 %)	36 (36 %)
3	'AB' +ve	3 (6 %)	6 (6 %)
4	'O' +ve	20 (40 %)	33 (33 %)
5	'A' –ve	1 (2 %)	0
6	'B' –ve	1 (2 %)	1 (1 %)
7	'AB' –ve	0	0
8	'O' -ve	3 (6 %)	2 (2 %)
TOTAL		**50 Boys**	**100 Girls**

Table – 4: Parental matching of Blood group between the Parents and Children in Class wise

S. No	Class	Parental matching of Blood group		
		Father's Blood Group Matching	Mother's Blood Group Matching	Not matching with Father and Mother Blood group
1	I B.Sc Biochemistry	21	21	4
2	II B.Sc Biochemistry	7	24	5
3	III B.Sc Biochemistry	9	16	2
4	I M.Sc Biochemistry	6	8	1
5	II M.Sc Biochemistry	2	12	0
6	PGDMLT	1	7	4
	TOTAL	**48 Students**	**86 Students**	**16 Students**

4.5. GENDER WISE PARENTAL MATCHING OF BLOOD GROUP BETWEEN THE PARENTS AND CHILDREN

Gender wise Parental matching of Blood group between the Parents and Children was surveyed in the present study and the data was given in Table – 5. We observed that, most of the Female student blood groups are matched with their Father's blood group (Male – 20 %; Female – 38 %). Reversely, Male student blood groups are matched with their Mother's blood group (Male – 72 %; Female – 50 %). In male student, 8 % of students are neutral and their blood group was not matched with their Father and Mother blood group. Likewise, 12 % of female students have showed neutral matching of Blood group and their blood group also not matched with their Father and Mother blood group.

Table – 5: Gender wise Parental matching of Blood group between the Parents and Children

S. No	Class	Father's Blood Group Matching	Mother's Blood Group Matching	Not matching with Father and Mother Blood group
1	I B.Sc Biochemistry	Male – 4 Female - 17	Male – 8 Female – 13	Male – 1 Female – 3
2	II B.Sc Biochemistry	Male – 3 Female – 4	Male – 11 Female – 13	Male – 2 Female – 3
3	III B.Sc Biochemistry	Male – 2 Female – 9	Male – 6 Female – 8	Male – 0 Female – 2
4	I M.Sc Biochemistry	Male – 1 Female – 5	Male – 2 Female – 6	Male – 0 Female – 1
5	II M.Sc Biochemistry	Male – 0 Female – 2	Male – 8 Female – 4	Male – 0 Female – 0
6	PGDMLT	Male – 0 Female – 1	Male – 1 Female – 6	Male – 1 Female – 3
	TOTAL	**Male – 10 (20 %)** **Female – 38 (38 %)**	**Male – 36 (72 %)** **Female – 50 (50 %)**	**Male – 4 (8 %)** **Female - 12 (12 %)**

5
CONCLUSION

From this present survey, we concluded that

- Among the eight Blood groups, maximum recorded Blood group among the Biochemistry department students was "O - Positive".

- Positive Rh Typing of Blood groups are observed more among the students when compared to the Positive Rh Typing Blood groups.

- For male students, highest percentage of Blood group was recorded as "O – Positive" and for Female students, highest percentage of Blood group was recorded as "B – Positive".

- Among the 150 surveyed Biochemistry students, 88 student blood group are matched with Mother's blood group, 46 student blood group are matched with Father's blood group and 16 student blood group are neutral not matched with their parents blood group.

- Most of the Female student blood groups are matched with their Father's blood group. Reversely, Male student blood groups are matched with their Mother's blood group.

6
REFERENCES

1) Agarwal N, Thapliyal RM and Chatterjee K. 2013. Blood group phenotype frequencies in blood donors from a tertiary care hospital in north India. *Blood Research*, 48: 51- 54.

2) Anstee DJ. 2010. The relationship between blood groups and disease. *Blood*, 115: 4635 - 4643.

3) Anstee DJ. 2011. The functional importance of blood group active molecules in human red blood cells. *Vox Sang*, 100: 140 - 149.

4) Choudhury P, Chakrabarti JS, Choudhury PS and Mail I. 2014. Frequency and distribution of blood groups in blood donors of Tripura. *Health*, 2(2): 57 - 61.

5) Cooper NR, Jensen FC, Welsh RM and Oldstone MB. 2016. Lysis of RNA tumor viruses by human serum: direct antibody-independent triggering of the classical complement pathway. *Journal of Experimental Medicine*, 144: 970 – 984.

6) Daniels G and Reid ME. 2010. Blood groups: The past 50 years. *Transfusion*, 50: 281 - 289.

7) Denomme GA. 2004. The structure and function of the molecules that carry human red blood cell and platelet antigens. *Transfusion Medical Reviews*, 18: 203 - 231.

8) Eru E, Adeniyi O and Jogo A. 2014. Frequency distribution of ABO and Rhesus blood groups among newly admitted students of Benue State University Makurdi, Nigeria. *African Journal of Biomedical Research*, 17(1): 49 - 52.

9) Garg N, Singh DK, Tomar R and Singh B. 2015. Phenotype Prevalence of Blood Group Systems (ABO, Rh, Kell) in Voluntary, Healthy Donors-Experience of a Tertiary Care Hospital in Delhi, North India. *Journal of Blood Disorders and Transfusion*, 15 - 20.

10) Gates MA, Wolpin BM, Cramer DW, Hankinson SE and Tworoger SS. 2011. ABO blood group and incidence of epithelial ovarian cancer. *International Journal of Cancer*, 128: 482 - 486.

11) Ghirardo SF, Mohan I, Gomensoro A and Chorost MI. 2010. Routine preoperative typing and screening: A safeguard or a misuse of resources. *Journal of Hematology*, 14: 395 - 398.

12) Goldstein J, Siviglia G, Hurst R, Lenny L and Reich L. 1982. Group B erythrocytes enzymatically converted to group O survive normally in A, B, and O individuals. *Science*, 215: 168 - 170.

13) Goldstein J. 1998. Conversion of ABO blood groups. *Transfusion Medical Reviews*, 3: 206 - 212.

14) Hashemi Najafabadi S, Vasheghani Farahani E, Shojaosadati SA, Rasaee MJ, Armstrong JK and Moin M. 2006. A method to optimize PEG coating of red blood cells. *Bioconjugation Chemistry*, 17: 1288 - 1293.

15) Hiltunen LM, Laivuori H, Rautanen A, Kaaja R, Kere J and Krusius T. 2009. Blood group AB and factor V Leiden as risk factors for pre-eclampsia: A population based nested case control study. *Thrombin Research*, 124: 167 - 173.

16) Kapadia A, Feizi T, Jewell D, Keeling J, Slavin G. 2011. Immunocytochemical studies of blood group A, H, I, and i antigens in gastric mucosae of infants with normal gastric histology and of patients with gastric carcinoma and chronic benign peptic ulceration. *Journal of Clinical Pathology*, 34: 320 - 237.

17) Kaur M, Singh A, Bassi R, Kaur H, Pezhman L and Sheikhzade F. 2011. Frequency and Distribution of Blood Groups among Medical Students of Sgrdimsar Amritsar. *Journal of Physiology*, 1(1): 1 - 25.

18) Kobayashi T, Liu D, Ogawa H, Miwa Y, Nagasaka T and Maruyama S. 2007. Alternative strategy for overcoming ABO incompatibility. *Transplantation*, 83: 1284 - 1286.

19) Liu QP, Sulzenbacher G, Yuan H, Bennett EP, Pietz G and Saunders K. 2007. Bacterial glycosidases for the production of universal red blood cells. *Natural Biotechnology*, 25: 454 - 464.

20) Lögdberg L, Reid ME and Zelinski T. 2011. Human blood group genes 2010: Chromosomal locations and cloning strategies revisited. *Transfusion Medical Reviews*, 25: 36 - 46.

21) Logdberg L, Reid ME, Lamont RE and Zelinski T. Human blood group genes. 2005. Chromosomal locations and cloning strategies. *Transfusion Medical Reviews*, 19: 45 - 57.

22) Luo H, Chaudhuri A, Zbrzezna V, He Y and Pogo AO. 2000. Deletion of the murine Duffy gene (Dfy) reveals that the Duffy receptor is functionally redundant. *Molecular Cell Biology*, 20: 3097 - 3101.

23) Miller RD. 2010. Transfusion therapy. In: Miller RD, Ericksson LI, Fleischer LA, Weiner - Kronish JP, Young LA, editors. Miller's Anesthesia. 7th ed. Philadelphia: Churchill Livingstone Elsevier; 1739 - 1766.

24) Onotai L and Lilly - Tariah OD. 2013. Adenoid and tonsil surgeries in children: How relevant is pre-operative blood grouping and cross - matching? *African Journal of Pediatrics Surgery*, 10: 231 - 234.

25) Owen R. 2000. Karl Landsteiner and the first human marker locus. *Genetics*, 155: 995 - 958.

26) Qadir MI and Malik SA. 2010. Comparison of alterations in red blood cell count and alterations in hemoglobin concentration in patients suffering from rectal carcinoma undergoing 5-fluorouracil and folic acid therapy. *Pharmacology Online*, 3: 240 - 243.

27) Rao N, Ferguson DJ, Lee SF and Telen MJ. 1991. Identification of human erythrocyte blood group antigens on the C3b/C4b receptor. *Journal of Immunology*, 146: 3502 - 3507.

28) Seltsam A, Hallensleben M, Kollmann A, Burkhart J and Blasczyk R. 2003. Systematic analysis of the *ABO* gene diversity within exons 6 and 7 by PCR screening reveals new *ABO* alleles. *Transfusion*, 43: 428 - 439.

29) Sun CF, Yu LC and Chen IP. 2003. Molecular genetic analysis for the *Ael* and *A3* alleles. *Transfusion*, 43:1138 - 1144.

30) Telen MJ, Hall SE, Green AM, Moulds JJ and Rosse WF. 1988. Identification of human erythrocyte blood group antigens on decay accelerating factor (DAF) and an erythrocyte phenotype negative for DAF. *Journal of Experimental Medicine*, 167: 1993 - 1998.

31) Tufano A, Coppola A, Nardo A, Bonfanti C, Crestani S and Cerbone AM. 2013. Non-O blood group as a risk factor for cerebral vein thrombosis. *International Journal of Thrombin Haemostat*, 110: 197 - 199.

32) Wang DS, Chen DL, Ren C, Wang ZQ, Qiu MZ and Luo HY. 2012. ABO blood group, hepatitis B viral infection and risk of pancreatic cancer. *International Journal of Cancer*, 131: 461 - 468.

33) Westhoff CM. 2004. The Rh blood group system in review: A new face for the next decade. *Transfusion*, 44: 1663 - 1673.

34) Wiggins KL, Smith NL, Glazer NL, Rosendaal FR, Heckbert SR and Psaty BM. 2009. ABO genotype and risk of thrombotic events and hemorrhagic stroke. *International Journal of Thrombin Haemostat*, 7: 263 - 269.

35) Zhang H, Mooney CJ and Reilly MP. 2012. ABO Blood Groups and Cardiovascular Diseases. *International Journal of Vascular Medicine*, 20: 641 - 645.

www.ingramcontent.com/pod-product-compliance
Lightning Source LLC
LaVergne TN
LVHW071700180726
843512LV00002B/502